Pain to Numbness to Healing

A
Collection of poems
by
Rosecursy Jean Baptiste

Copyright © 2011 by Rosecursy Jean Baptiste

All rights reserved. This book or any portion thereof may not be reproduced or used in any manner whatsoever without the express written permission of the publisher except for the use of brief quotations in a book review.

Rosecursy Jean Baptiste
1509 Alcott Street
Philadelphia PA 19149

Printed in the United States of America

First Printing: September 2011

ISBN 978-1-105-10151-9

Pain
to
Numbness
to
Healing

Giving Honor to God

Looking unto Jesus the author and finisher of our faith; who for the joy that was set before him endured the cross, despising the shame, and is set down at the right hand of the throne of God.

Hebrews 12:2

Introduction

This book contains series of poems that timelines the heart from the state of brokenness and confusion to wholeness and completion. I use to write sad love songs. Everything I wrote was about complex emotions and deep wounds. Wounds that knew no healing. Wounds that held ugly scars. Wounds that was relieved by deeper ones. It was not until I found Jesus that I was able to sing a new song. Songs that uplifted my heart and transcended to others. Though I still have sad songs to sing, I have now come to a place where there is healing. A balm in Gilead! To mend my broken heart, to heal the wounds and erase the scars.

Rosecursy

I, Rosecursy to all,

cure see, to all that bothers your soul.

Try my love see the remedy of your Rose

So luscious don't let me wither,

leave my petals, let me bloom.

I, Rosecursy to all,

cure see, the pain you have to feel.

When the thorns of life stick you and then you bleed.

This red Rosecursy the red liquid that came from your cut.

And with that same thorn I cure.

See how it heals?

Feel the sweetness.

Only this Rosecursy could bring such cure.

So leave my petals, let me bloom and don't let me wither

I Rosecursy to all

cure see, what just isn't right.

I can stand alone, have HIM by my side and cure what you can't endure.

And I do this with my Lord

JESUS

I, Rosecursy!

In loving memory of

The old me

Give me a different kind of Pain

Hush!

Oh, I know this pain is too much to bear.

Just lay me down and let me sleep,

until the pain can't be felt any longer.

Rip out my insides, especially the heart,

so it can't pump love through my veins.

I don't want to feel. I don't want to care.

And I surely don't want to cry,

so destroy my tear ducts so water won't drip

Hush!

Hush, and I know this pain is too much

Rather lay and sleep until the pain is gone

Crack my skull and shred my brain.

Kill the cells that's full of thought

so I can't think

Shrink my cerebrum to lesson my emotions.

*Memory would be so faint that I won't
remember such things as pain.
Hush!
I know this pain is too much to feel
Fry my nerves so I could become paralyzed.
Movement can't be made so I would
lay here and sleep.
I would meditate on death's sweetness and
dreams would play and impair my pain
that hurts the most.
Don't forget to cut up my body so the hurt
pieces are small then it would
be so much easier to swallow.
Hush!
I know this pain can't bear.
So throw away the skin so no remains of
bitterness could be eaten.*

Leave me with hair, that's already dead but still grows full of strength so pain is nothing and too weak to be felt.

Give me a different kind of pain.

Anything else so I won't have to bear or cope with this sorrow.

Hush!

Let me sleep until pain disappears

Hush!

When

Feels like hell sitting here wondering where my soul is at when my heart is gone.
Not knowing at all what to think or should I feel the possibility of things not right.
While thoughts wander and visions merge
To see what must've happen.
Presently seeking answers of unknown questions.
Leaving eyes wet and egos bruised
In search of why is this and why not that.
Yearning to know who, need to know the identity of the unspoken.
Love melting and hate freezing.
Battling for just have to be or couldn't be so.
Distracted by the past and blinded by the future.

Won't be long until fate comes at the wrong time.

Pondering

The mind is irritated when the body aches.

Measuring up to no maturity.

Explanation can't be told to sooth the soul.

Facing this alone.

I still can't take nobody with me.

Effort made to comfort useless appreciation.

To part with such easiness,

joining was way too hard.

When you trample this state of mind and try not to step on it, can't get out, won't get out or your way.

So you pick it up instead just to feel

what won't be ignored

Pondering on.

Times up!

What's the motive

Where we at?

Days go by too fast

that your body is late.

Eyes didn't even blink

Until time is up.

Fly High

Baby I'm high.

Yes, I'm up there.

Way too far to even care.

Lost in herbs full of analyzation.

Bring me higher

so I am much more.

Baby, I'm high

The air just went down my throat

I breathe it in and it lifts me up.

Nothing can reach me and

please don't try to pull me down.

Leave me up high so I could see beyond.

Baby, I'm high.

I'm so up there.

I choke and it provokes,

causing me to go where I want to be.
My lungs then inhale just to exhale
and air goes down my throat.
Upgrading my level but
slowing down my thoughts.
and I'm so high,
they can't reach me.
What will it take for me to come down?

Love never runs out of time

Love to love you baby

But you don't

Waiting patiently

I need your love

Counting the number of times the clock ticks

Never will run out of time

Let the days drag-on.

Transitioning

Should be a Gemini,

with the way I battle against both sides.

I want the wicked to win...

Wait!

My faith is too strong

I want to die

Wait!

I'm too full of life

I want to testify

Wait!

Where's my mony?

Who will win this battle that's not even mine?

Should be a fighter,

with the way I wrestle with the truth.

I struggle with the lies

Wait!

Nothing but truth faces me

I stand up to fall

Wait!

Finding my position.

Should be a baby,

with the way I cry,

My tears are dry.

Still I get by.

The process is worth a try.

As I

Transition from a girl

to a child

of

The Most High.

Shivers Down My Spine

Shivers down my spine.

I'm so glad you're mine.

Time seemed to roll fast.

I'm just hoping this will last.

As you break through the shields

that barricades my heart.

You're healing the wounds that pierced with

thorns of love I thought I had.

The rose pedals fall and the flower blooms.

Like those flowers I need you

my sun, my light.

But darkness soon rise and my sun will be gone

I wait for the time to roll fast

Hoping, please just last

and rise again my sun so I can feel

shivers down my spine

Please, please be mine

Fill my stems with sweet fluids

Shower me with the power to love.

To love and endure.

My sun, my light sends

shivers down my spine

Why not be mine?

To Success

Control to do what I could.

Not a bit of fear in my heart.

Wicked as could be and oh so bold.

Go about to do things that should be done.

Stepping down to climb up top.

Backing up to move forward.

See the power that one possesses.

Control to do what I could.

Underneath I lay no longer.

Slip from that to reach further.

Goals that need to be scored.

Achievements that need to be achieved.

Wishing too hard

I inhale hoping this will cease my pain

Just for a little while.

Just until I can cope.

Pondering on my wrongs and just not rights.

Another breath brings me closer to what I fail to see.

Too many wishes went ungranted

so there's no reason to wish more.

What joke?

Seem to be no hope.

Longing for the right time that comes once in a lifetime.

Struck by sadness that will ever overcome.

Won't complain because there must be a reason

Refuse to cry because it's just my fault.

Never will give up, then what's the worth.

Content with nothing, it won't hurt when it's gone.

Fixed ideas rearrange and now needs to be fixed

Can't laugh to what's not funny.

Cuz!

Cuz, that's what I do sometimes,

I speak my mind cuz I should.

That's what I do.

Tear you apart,

put you together,

cuz I can't bare what I've done.

Try so many times to let go

cuz it might not be worth it.

A simple thought ambushes the brain

cuz reactions tend to backfire

and I wonder why it is that I do

what I do sometimes.

Cuz that's what I do

when I do what I do sometimes.

Catalyze your cells then I anatomize.

Eat you away just to spit you out

and bring you to the same state.

That's what I do sometimes.

Cuz I refuse to be torn down like I do you

when I do what I do sometimes.

I do the demolition and destruct all walls just to rebuild.

Knock all odds, stay even and straighten

what is crooked even though I made it slant.

That's what I do sometimes.

Just cuz.

Speak!

As the heart pounds

As the lungs expands

And the blood flows

And the neurons transmit

Lie Still

While the air moves

And the water waves

And the atoms mix

Plus matter does take space

Lie Still

So the eyes see

And the ears hear

And the senses sense

Plus the soul does feel

Lie Still

Til the rose bloom

And the roots grow

And the petals sweat

Plus the thorns do cut

Lie still

Let the tongue taste

And the buds sting

And the teeth clench

Plus the mouth does speak

Lie Still.

The way I feel

Lovely when I'm powdered

and smelling like sweetness.

Dressed to impress and eyes rest

confirms I look the best.

Happy when receiving soft kisses

which never misses

that hard spot in my chest.

Charmed when bright smile releases

expressions of joy that feeds back

my humor when you want more.

Tired when long days

are followed by long nights.

Upset when things won't go my way.

Revengeful when you cross me.

Excited when it catches my interest.

Generous when I got it like that.

Relaxed because everything happens for a reason and will reap in due season.

Uptight because I should've been there.

Lost when I can't find my way.

Devastated because you told me that lie.

Not impressed when you confessed.

Overwhelmed when there's just too much

Deprived when there's not enough.

Spoiled when I get the right gift.

Blessed when I feel no stress.

Sundays

Time with family that we dread to give.

Effort to care that usually peeve

Bonding of sorts that we pull apart

Late wake ups or early mornings,

to start a day full of nothing or

to end and give up everything.

To some tradition, others regular.

Different minds play on Sundays.

The day of rest or begin the week

The point of busyness or the day of ease

To go away or return home

All day in bed or dancing praises

Humble and quiet or cheerful and loud

Different people do different things on Sundays

Cutting coupons or reading late news

Reciting poetry or gospel tunes

The sound of birds making love or

the bark of dogs fighting for food.

What I do on my Sundays

is pray, pray, pray and

try not to act like a fool.

Free!

A prisoner with the key

is useless if there's no lock.

To have authority and no commandments

is also useless.

To walk in light with a heart full of darkness

is destruction to the soul.

To live in the world is deadly

but to live in God is freedom.

His Holy Spirit will brighten our hearts

and strengthen our souls.

His commandments must be followed with authority.

Would you need a key when you already

free.

Thanks

Thanks to the giving that may not want to give

Hope to receive what's not deserved.

Chance to accept all that is due.

Tomorrow could be new.

Thanks to the kindness given with no charm,

For the short breaths and long goodbyes,

For yesterday that may not be gone,

For today though I wish it was not here.

Thanks oh Lord for what I do not have.